HISTORY OF

EIGHTH EDITION

History of the Theatre